PlayPRAISE
Most Requested

9 Piano Arrangements of Contemporary Worship Songs
Arranged by Tom Gerou & Victor Labenske

In the *PlayPRAISE* series, pianists young and old will find accessible arrangements of some of the best in contemporary Christian praise and worship music. These tunes have become a familiar part of the musical fabric of contemporary praise worship.

It is best for piano students to observe the rhythms as notated, but these may be adjusted later to match what they have heard at church.

The joy found in learning these arrangements will result in performers who want to continue to *PlayPRAISE*.

ISBN-10: 0-7390-4909-7
ISBN-13: 978-0-7390-4909-9

Alfred

The Wonderful Cross

Words and Music by Isaac Watts, Jesse Reeves,
Chris Tomlin, and J. D. Walt
Arr. by Tom Gerou and Victor Labenske

come and die___ and find___ that I___ may tru - ly live.___

O the won - der - ful cross, O the

won - der - ful cross bids me come and die___ and find___

___ that I___ may tru - ly live.___ *dim. poco a poco*

rit. *p*

8va

We Fall Down

Words and Music by Chris Tomlin
Arr. by Tom Gerou and Victor Labenske

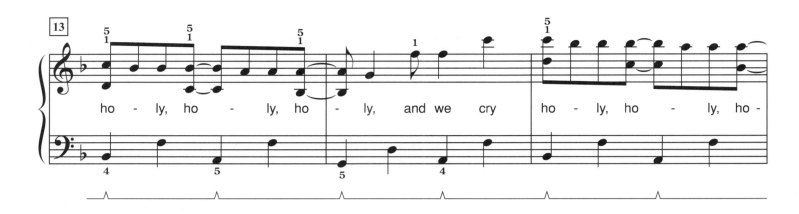

ho - ly, ho - ly, ho - ly, and we cry ho - ly, ho - ly, ho -

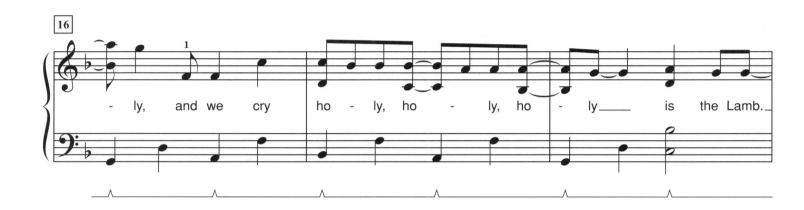

- ly, and we cry ho - ly, ho - ly, ho - ly____ is the Lamb.

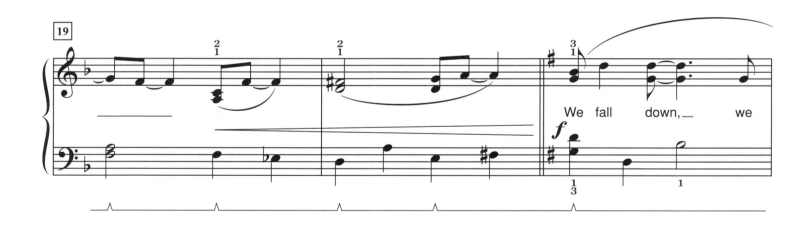

_____ We fall down,__ we

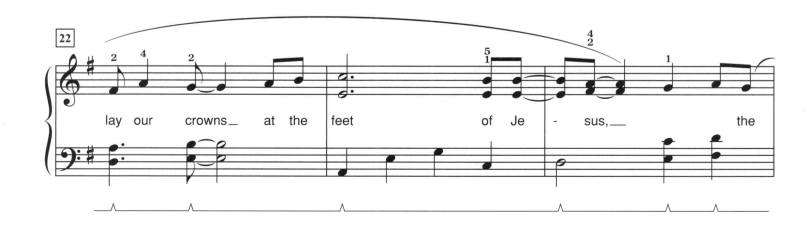

lay our crowns__ at the feet of Je - sus,__ the

greatness of____ mer - cy and love___ at the feet of Je -

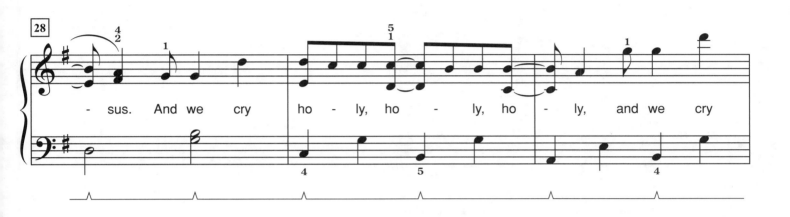

- sus. And we cry ho - ly, ho - ly, ho - ly, and we cry

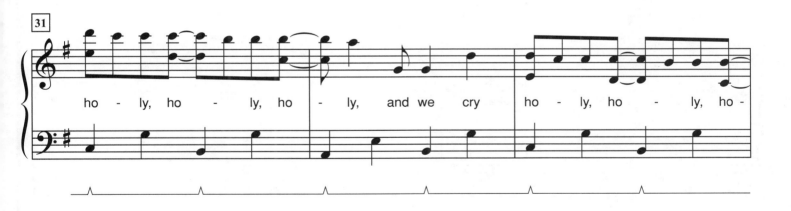

ho - ly, ho - ly, ho - ly, and we cry ho - ly, ho - ly, ho -

- ly___ is the Lamb.___ *dim.* *rit.* *mp*

Sanctuary

Words and Music by
John W. Thompson and Randy Scruggs
Arr. by Tom Gerou and Victor Labenske

Indescribable

Words and Music by Jesse Reeves and Laura Story
Arr. by Tom Gerou and Victor Labenske

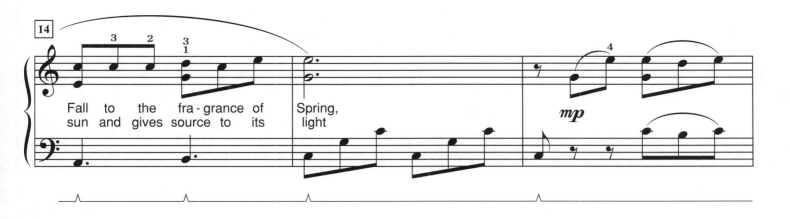

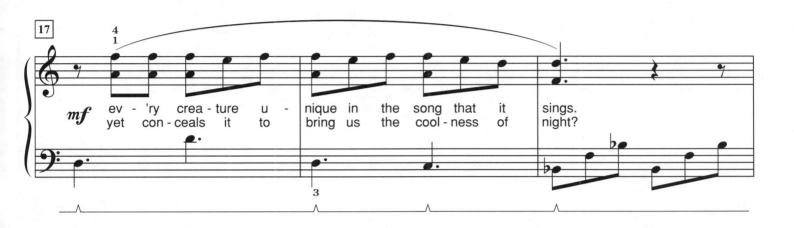

Lord Reign in Me

Words and Music by Brenton Brown
Arr. by Tom Gerou and Victor Labenske

Rock beat (♩ = 108)

O - ver all the earth, You reign on high, ev - 'ry moun - tain stream, ev - 'ry sun - set sky. But my one re - quest, Lord, my on - ly aim is that You'd

reign in me a-gain. Lord, reign in me, reign in Your pow'r,

O-ver all my dreams in my dark-est hour. You are the Lord

of all I am, so won't You reign in me a-gain.

mp *f* Lord, reign in me,

Blessed Be Your Name

Words and Music by Matt Redman and Beth Redman
Arr. by Tom Gerou and Victor Labenske

praise. When the dark - ness clos - es in, Lord,

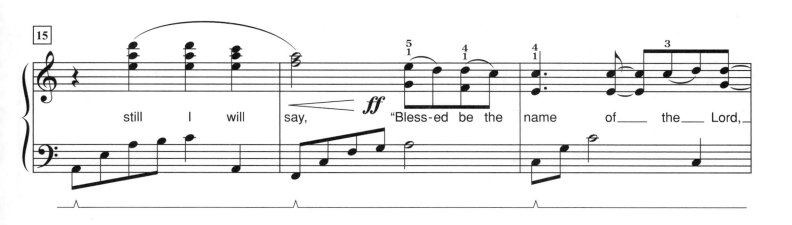

still I will say, *ff* "Bless-ed be the name of ___ the ___ Lord,

___ bless-ed be Your name. Bless-ed be the

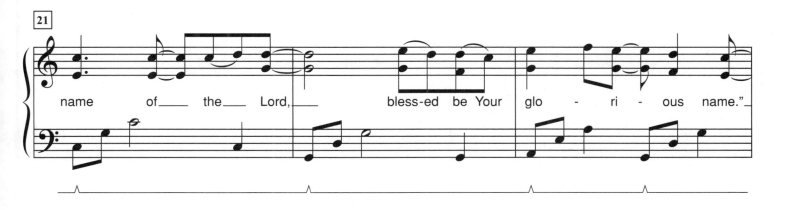

name of ___ the ___ Lord, ___ bless-ed be Your glo - ri - ous name."

Beautiful One

Words and Music by Tim Hughes
Arr. by Tom Gerou and Victor Labenske

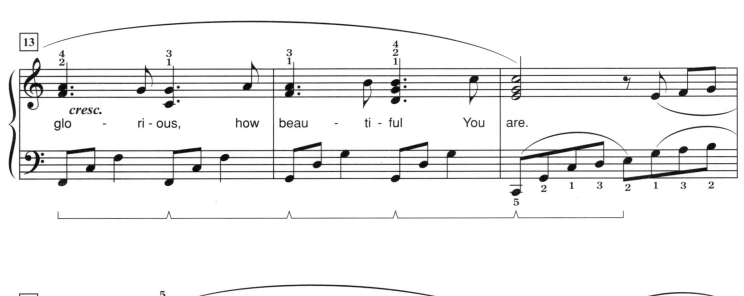

glo - ri - ous, how beau - ti - ful You are.

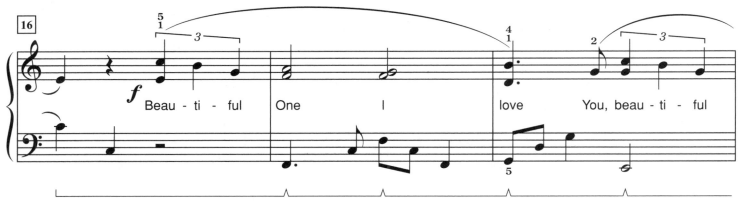

Beau - ti - ful One I love You, beau - ti - ful

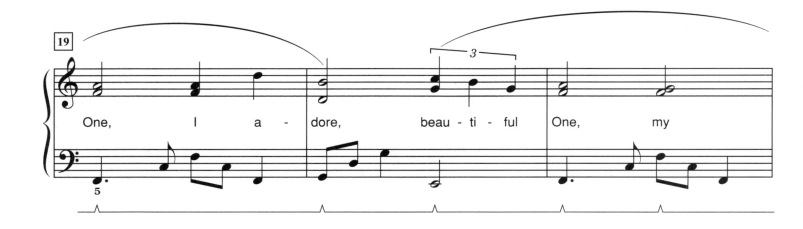

One, I a - dore, beau - ti - ful One, my

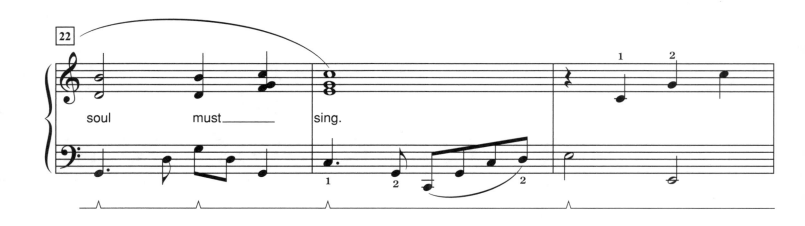

soul must_____ sing.

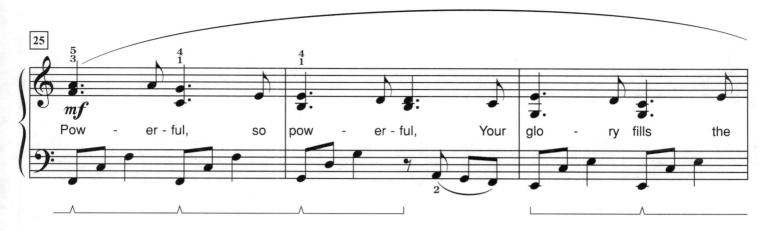

Pow - er - ful, so pow - er - ful, Your glo - ry fills the

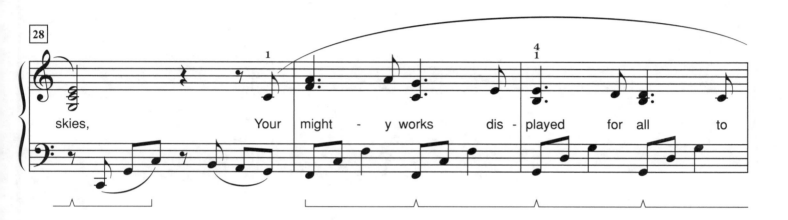

skies, Your might - y works dis - played for all to

see. The beau - ty of Your

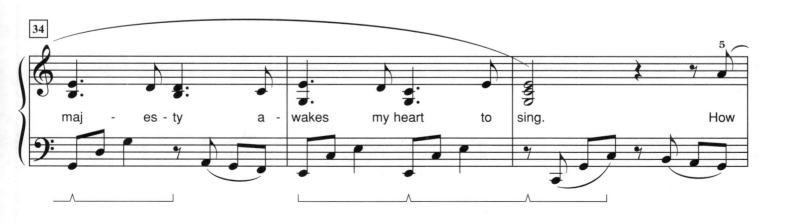

maj - es - ty a - wakes my heart to sing. How

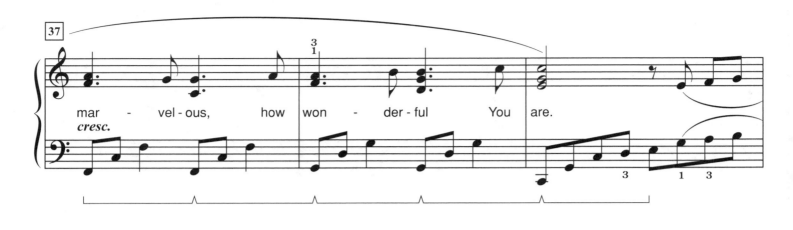

mar - vel - ous, how won - der - ful You are.

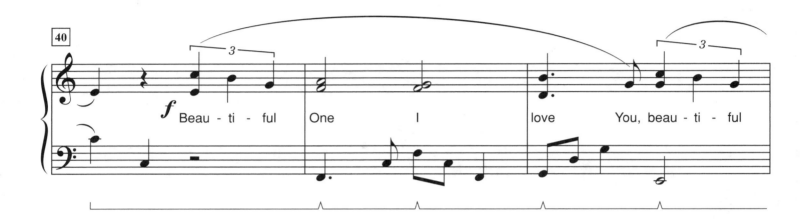

Beau - ti - ful One I love You, beau - ti - ful

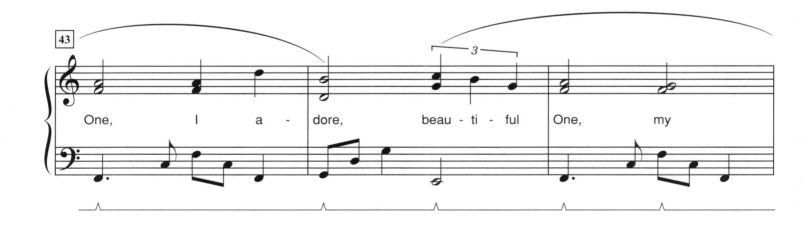

One, I a - dore, beau - ti - ful One, my

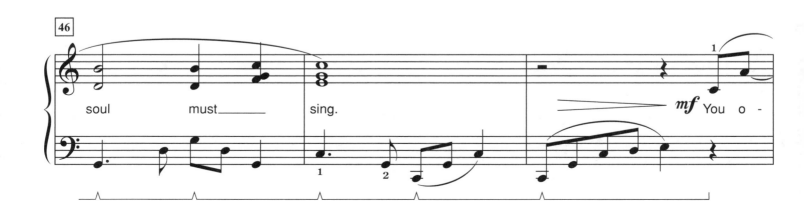

soul must___ sing. You o -

You're Worthy of My Praise

Words and Music by David Ruis
Arr. by Tom Gerou and Victor Labenske

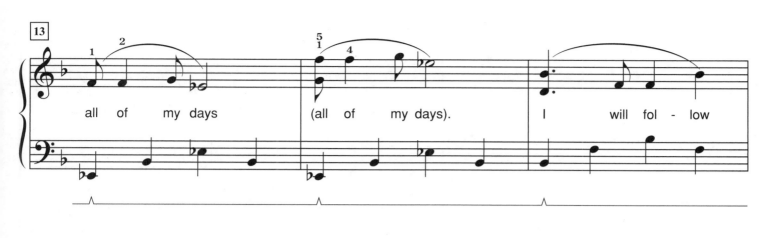

all of my days (all of my days). I will fol - low

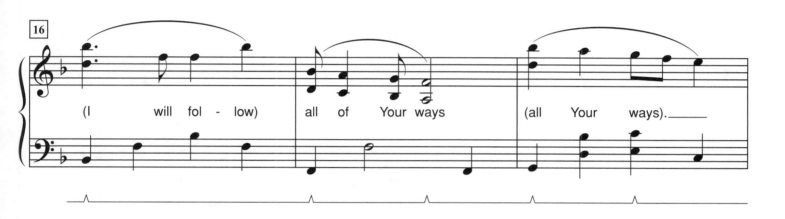

(I will fol - low) all of Your ways (all Your ways).___

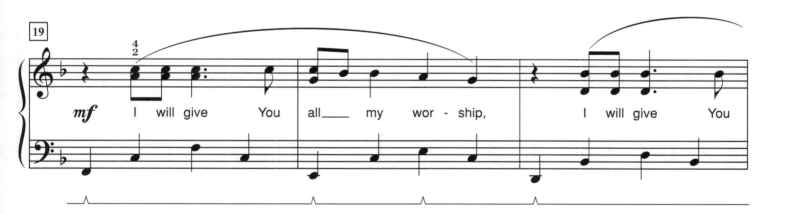

mf I will give You all___ my wor - ship, I will give You

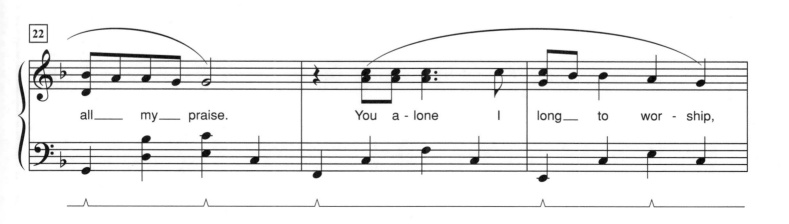

all___ my___ praise. You a - lone I long___ to wor - ship,

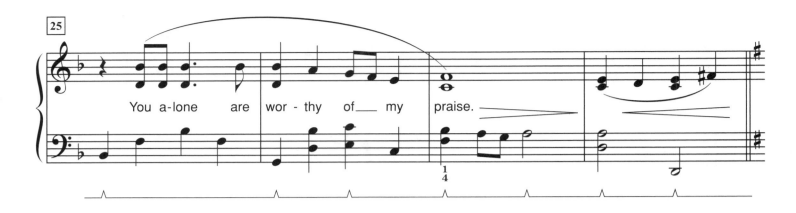

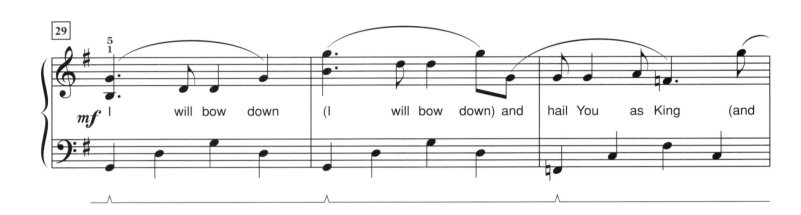

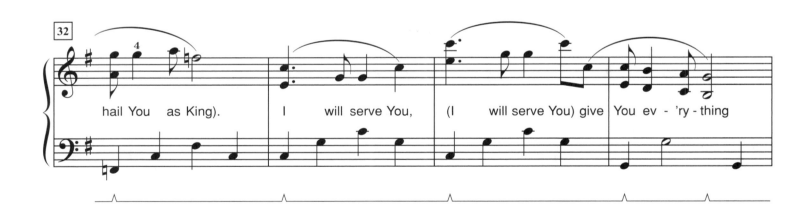

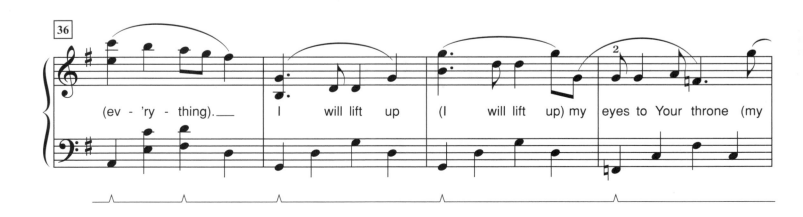

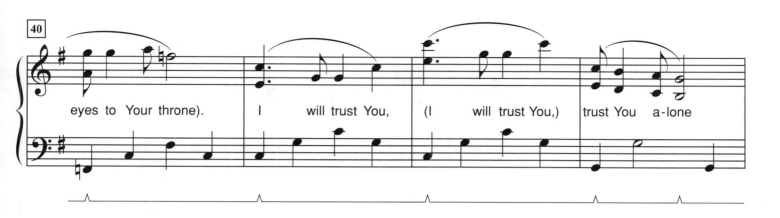

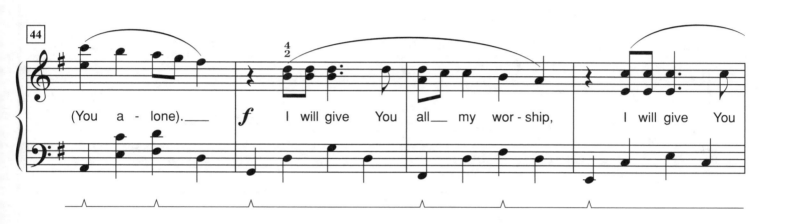

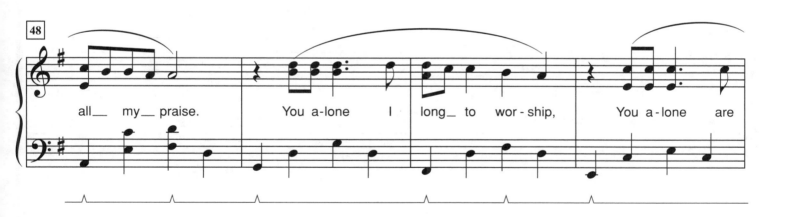

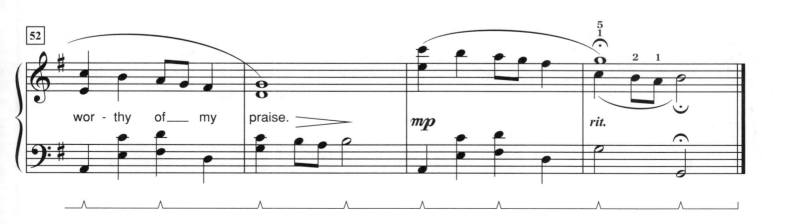

Holy Is The Lord

Words and Music by Chris Tomlin and Louie Giglio
Arr. by Tom Gerou and Victor Labenske

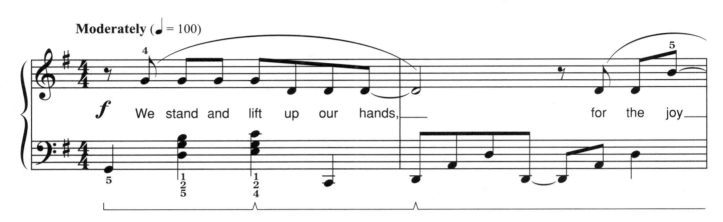

We stand and lift up our hands, for the joy

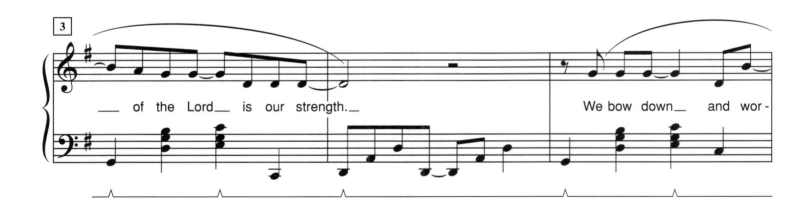

of the Lord is our strength. We bow down and wor-

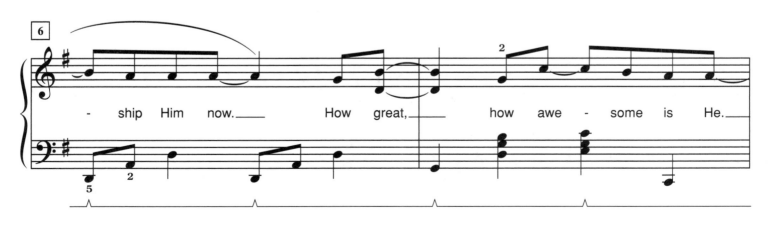

-ship Him now. How great, how awe-some is He.

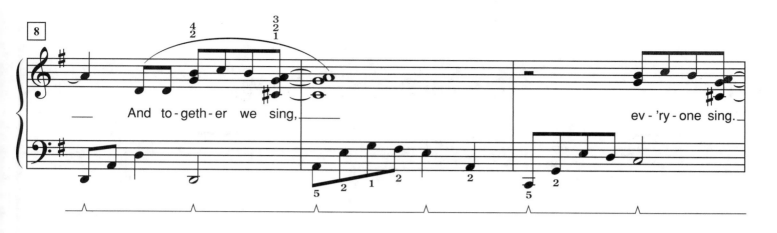

And to-geth-er we sing, ev-'ry-one sing.

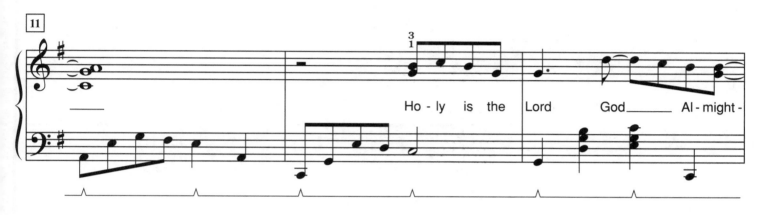

Ho-ly is the Lord God Al-might-

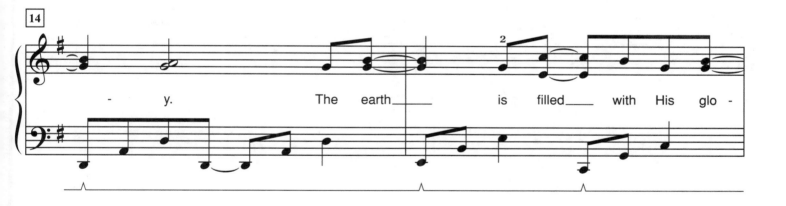

-y. The earth is filled with His glo-

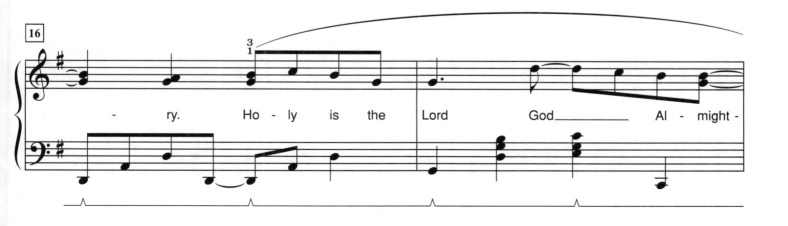

-ry. Ho-ly is the Lord God Al-might-

-y. The earth___ is filled__ with His glo - ry. The earth

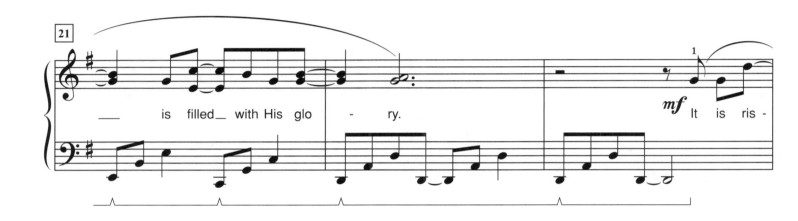

___ is filled__ with His glo - ry. *mf* It is ris -

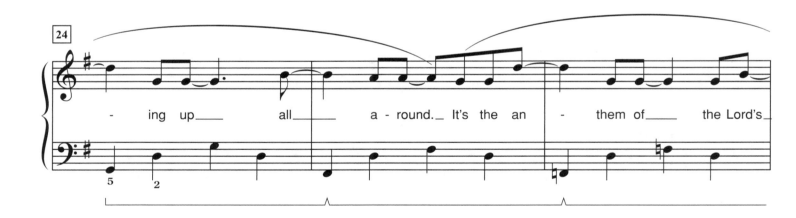

- ing up___ all___ a - round._ It's the an - them of___ the Lord's

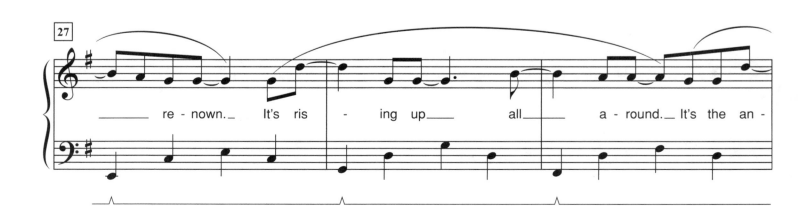

___ re - nown._ It's ris - ing up___ all___ a - round._ It's the an -

them of ___ the Lord's ___ re - nown. ___ *cresc.* And to - geth - er we sing,

f ___ ev - 'ry - one sing. ___

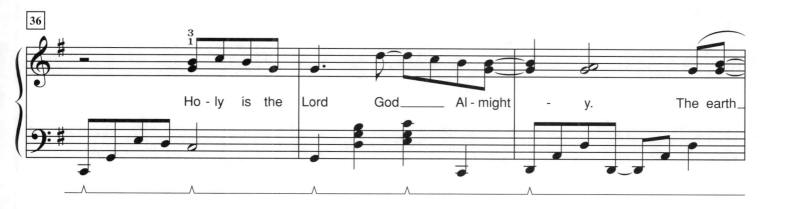

Ho - ly is the Lord God ___ Al - might - y. The earth ___

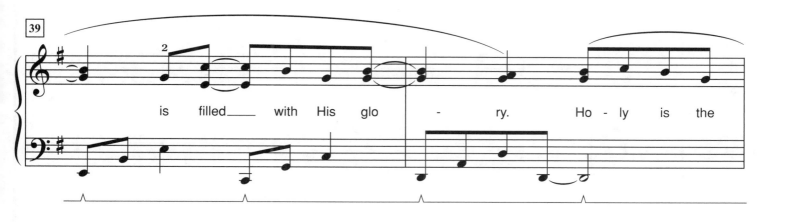

is filled ___ with His glo - ry. Ho - ly is the

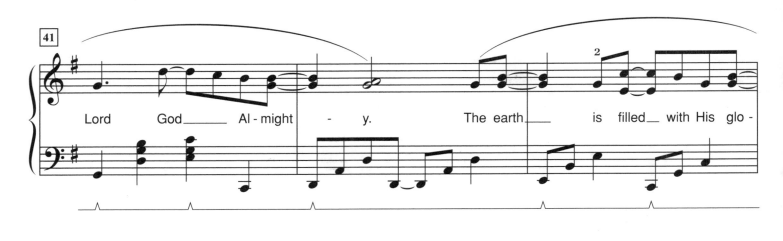

Lord God_____ Al - might - - y. The earth____ is filled__ with His glo -

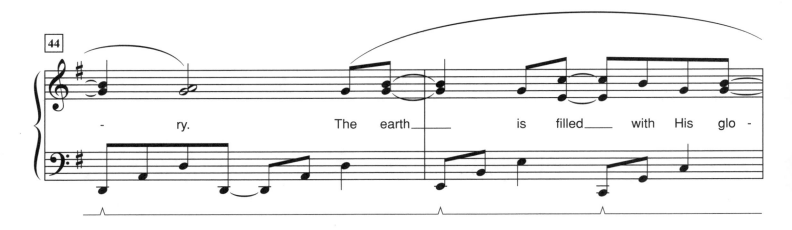

- ry. The earth____ is filled____ with His glo -

- ry. The earth____ is filled__ with His glo - ry._____

mf *rit.*